The Five N.   _ _u!as

BUDDHA'S TEACHING
of the
FIVE HINDRANCES

The obstacles to
SEEING the TRUTH
&
Putting an
END
to
SUFFERING

Brian Taylor

UNIVERSAL OCTOPUS

Other Publications in the Same Series:

What is Buddhism?
Buddhism and Drugs
The Five Buddhist Precepts
Basic Buddhist Meditation
The Living Waters of Buddhism
Basic Buddhism for a World in Trouble
Dependent Origination (*Paṭiccasamuppāda*)
The Ten Fetters (*Saŋyojana*)
Buddhist Pali Chants with English Translations

Published by Universal Octopus 2017
www.univeraloctopus.com

ISBN 978-0-9956346-8-8

The Buddha left home at 29. He was a prince, heir to a small Kingdom and married with a son. He was in the prime of life.

Then, it is said, he saw the "four signs". An old man, a sick man, a corpse being carried to cremation and a monk in meditation beneath a tree.

This focused his mind on old age, disease, and death, the universal characteristics which are present in every human life, no matter how princely and well-endowed.

Dissatisfaction arose in him, which no changes to his life-style could abolish, so long as these characteristics remained.

The monk in meditation beneath a tree made him realise he was not alone in his realisation. Others, too, had become disenchanted with the impermanence and ultimate unsatisfactoriness of Life and were trying to find a way out.

In every generation, there have been many who have experienced the same profound disillusion. Mostly, they have tried to improve the quality of their temporary lives, "making the most of" Life as they found it. Or, if their disillusion goes deeper, they have continued their search for Truth within the comfortable confines of their society; its colleges, schools, libraries and monasteries.

Few, like this Prince, have been so serious as to give up status, friends, wealth, family, home and even the clothes off their backs to go off in search of the Deathless.

Of those who have done so, how many have succeeded?

The Prince, himself, visited the wise men of his time and place, such as Alara and Udaka. He listened to their teachings. He put them into practice. He attained what they had attained. Each offered him the position of joint teacher. He declined. He was still not satisfied.

After six years of ascetic practices, he finally achieved the goal he had set himself and devised a method and techniques by which those who wanted to follow in his footsteps could (and can) tread the Path. From then on, he was called Buddha, the "Awakened One".

Awakened to what?

To the unsatisfactoriness of Life as we experience it from birth to death.

What Goal?

Freedom from everything that is unsatisfactory, including Death.

What Path?

The Path to Freedom.

The Fourth Noble Truth

Right Seeing
Right Thought
Right Speech
Right Action
Right Livelihood
Right Effort
Right Mindfulness
Right Concentration

This Path is intended to assist an honest and straight-forward man who pursues Truth for its own sake and not just for his personal advantage.

He is able to grasp and puts into practice the fundamental Ethic,

Not doing to other living beings what you would not wish to be done to you.

Central to the successful treading of this Path is bringing the mind under control. It can then be purified and becomes a useful tool rather than an unreliable master.

This leads, as a knock-on effect, to purification of thought, speech and bodily activities. This normalises one's relations with other living beings and the world in which we and they live.

The Hindrances

Buddha identified Five Nivāraṇas (Hindrances or Blockages), which prevent us from seeing the Truth about ourselves and the world around us.

Kāma-Chanda: Sensory Desire
Vyāpāda: Ill-will
Thīna-Middha: Sloth and Torpor
Uddhacca-Kukkucca: Restlessness and Regret
Vicikicchā: Doubt

They also stand in the way of our being able to experience the freedom of Nibbāna for ourselves.

One or more of these obstacles is present at every stage of the Path until the ultimate attainment of the Arahant - the Deathless.

These Hindrances affect the senses. The senses are the fundamentals of Life itself.

The Senses

The function of our five external senses is to provide conscious access to the outside world into which we have been born.

It is as though we turn up in a spaceship on an alien planet which, in many ways, is what we do.

We come equipped to explore our new world.

Eyes: Windows to see the landscape
Ears: Microphones to detect sounds
Nose: Ventilator to test the air quality
Tongue: Instrument to test for food
Skin: Membrane of external sensors to register heat and cold, pressure and invasion.

Stripped to the essentials, being born as a human being starts out very much like this.

The number and range of external senses varies considerably among the different classes of beings. The more external senses we have, the more comprehensive our perception of the external world will be.

Think of the different "worlds" as perceived by earthworms, eagles, blind men, deaf men, butterflies, intestinal worms, coelacanths etc.

The Sixth Sense

We also bring with us an on-board computer (Mind) to analyse the data the senses collect and tell us how to react. Or even to tell us that our best chance of survival is to leave at once and go back where we came from! (Cot deaths? "Those whom the Gods love, die young." ...etc.)

Our reactions, thoughts, words and deeds are conditioned by the interpretation put upon the external sense-data by this sixth sense - the mind. These interpretations are programmed to enable us to react in ways which maximise our chances of survival and minimise our chances of non-survival.

The more complex the sixth sense is the more complex our reactions will be.

But not necessarily the more accurate. For this is where the Hindrances can put in their appearance.

The Source of the Hindrances

Our sixth sense may and does go beyond just providing data relevant to survival and non-survival and, instead, introduces a tendency for preferences: likes and dislikes, pleasures and displeasures.

The complex then becomes the complicated. Our perceptions of the world become distorted by our minds and may actually give rise to reactions that are non-survival.

Example?

Alcohol is a stimulant and a poison. Like it, it's nice. Like it too much, you may become addicted to it. It then becomes a Must-have-it, a Can't-do-without-it. Then, you may end up "literally" drinking yourself to death. An obvious case of non-survival.

The way the Hindrances work is seen very clearly in the first two.

Sensory Desire and Ill-will make a pair. They are opposites.

But not in the same way that Desire and No Desire are opposites.

Where Desire is the opposite of No Desire, it is in the sense that Desire is the opposite of Freedom from Compulsive Desire.

This is the discovery that can lead to Liberation from Suffering. No desire, ultimately no suffering.

Absolute Freedom from Suffering is the goal of humanity, whether it realises it or not.

As far as the Hindrances are concerned, what Sensory Desire and Ill-will have in common is that they both hinder us from achieving this Freedom from Suffering.

Both are active emotions, outward movements from the mind of energy and feeling.

But they are opposite kinds of emotion.

They are opposites in the sense that hot water is the opposite of cold water. Certainly, hot is the opposite of cold. But both are water, flowing from the water tap.

If you want to put an end to hot and cold water, you have to turn off the water at the tap.

If you want to put an end to Desire and Ill-will, you have to turn off that outward-reaching energy from the mind tap, where it is alternately pulling in its likes in order to grasp them; or grasping its dislikes in order to push them away and reject them.

Survival

In its uncontaminated form, this outward moving energy, is simply exploratory, concerned with survival. We see this very clearly in animals.

But, as part of the exploratory activities of the senses, Consciousness triggers Feeling.

Pro-survival awareness is felt as liking and non-survival as disliking. This need not be a problem. Consider the procreation of the species, which is obviously pro-survival. Or the good taste of wholesome food.

But it can develop into preference and aversion. It then links with the future and the past. This tendency spreads and accumulates until the original, natural, protective reaction to phenomena, perceived at the sense doors, is taken over by wanting and aversion.

To the extent that one identifies with the body and the mind, the phenomena then become inseparably linked to I, Me, and Mine. The Ego.

The Ego

The Buddha lists this False Identification among the Ten Fetters (Saṇyojana) at number eight. It is Māna, the giving rise to a false idea of a separate self.

The Fetters (Saŋyojana)

Saŋyojana means "(mental) fetter, chain". A fetter is something that holds you as a prisoner, so that you lose your freedom and power to escape. Except in the case of masochists, fetters are usually applied by others.

In Buddhist psychology, it is shown that the mental Saŋyojanas are located <u>within</u> ourselves.

Escape is not, therefore, a matter of breaking free from the fetters but of letting go of our hold on them.

Fetters and Hindrances are just different ways of looking at the same thing.

We reach out to grab something because we want to hold on to it. But we also reach out to grab something in order to push it away or destroy it. Either way, we are (literally) stuck with it.

We reach out of our spaceship and grasp at the sense phenomena we have come to crave for.

Or we see them as fetters which grasp us and this leads to ill-will.

In both cases the process and result are the same. The fetter cannot grasp your hand if you don't reach towards it with your hand. Think of putting your hand between the bars to stroke the lion.

Suffering

All the hindrances result in Loss of Freedom and equanimity. Suffering.

"Now this, bhikkhus, is the noble truth of suffering: birth is suffering, aging is suffering, illness is suffering, death is suffering; being with what is displeasing is suffering; separation from what is pleasing is suffering; not to get what one wants is suffering; in brief, the five aggregates, subject to clinging, are suffering."

The Five Aggregates (khandhas)

The five aggregates are: forms, sensations, perceptions, mental formations and consciousness.

The Buddha asserts that these five factors constitute a living being's mental and physical existence and are, therefore, the basis for all our suffering.

Close examination of them in our life-continuum provides a continuous demonstration that there is to be found in mind and body, no trace of a permanent, enduring individual soul or self.

The gate to Freedom from Suffering is now wide open.

1. Kāma-Chanda: Sensory Desire

This is the desire (chanda) for

a) sense objects (kāma),
b) for the senses themselves, and
c) for the feelings experienced while using the senses.

It is that particular type of wanting which, when using the five senses of sight, sound, smell, taste and physical touch, is seeking for happiness rather than for information. Humans are currently more susceptible to this than animals.

We look out from our spaceship and get an overview of space and the objects it contains with our eyes. This gives us the lie of the land.

We turn up the microphone and use our ears and gather what information we can from interpreting sound waves.

The ventilator (nose) provides a sample of the air so that our computer can indicate whether or not it is safe to wind down the window and let it in.

The food taster/tester functions as the tongue.

Finally, the external sensors (skin) enable us to monitor the effect on our space ship of temperature and pressure from the moving and stationary objects, so that we know which ones to avoid.

All the while, our computer is working continuously with the inflow of data to organise and evaluate it in categories: pro-survival; anti-survival; neutral; don't know. And also memory.

This can be crucial. The computer is relating its findings to other information, stored on the hard drive, of previous visits to this or other planets in this or other spaceships!

Simply put, we see a location which, it seems, will protect our spaceship (us) from the objects around us and the weather. It does the job and we park ourselves there.

We can hear what goes on around us and we use this to our benefit. The lion sounds a bit close. We change our location.

We smell the plants and fruits and refer them to our tongues and taste buds to test their palatability.

We feel with our skins that the sun is too hot and we move into the shade. The rocks are too hard so we sit on the grass.

Our minds continuously calculate the pros and cons of location, food and environment and we use our free will to adjust and improve the circumstances of our lives and environment. All in the pursuit of Survival.

In this, we are doing what all the other living beings are doing, with varying degrees of consciousness.

To begin with, the cat shares a similar level of consciousness with us.

From the beginning and throughout its life, the tree does not. It behaves in a way that seems to us automatic or even unconscious.

However, there is no life without a certain degree of consciousness. Otherwise, it would not be alive.

Then, at some point, a complication arises when, instead of reacting automatically like all of the vegetable kingdom, or semi-automatically like most of the animal kingdom, we identify with our responses and the sense objects to which they relate.

Thoughts arise, "I like that!" "I don't like that!" We even use phrases such as "No, the colour's wrong. I don't think that's me!"

This is where the hindrance comes in. It prevents us from being objective in our perceptions and responses.

It starts with: *that's not good*;
superimposes: *I like it*;
moves on to: *it may be bad but I like it;*
then: *it's bad for me but I want it anyway*;
finally: *if I want it, it can't be bad for me.*

At this stage, the mind becomes skilled at distorting information so that it accommodates "my" likes and dislikes and filtering out whatever information doesn't suit me and my purposes.

It is then a fully-fledged hindrance standing between me and seeing the simple truth about anything. It is Avijjā, ignorance; not seeing what is obviously really there.

To rectify this, the Buddha starts his Noble Eightfold Path with:

1. Right View (sammā-diṭṭhi).

If alcohol is a poison and it's bad for you, see it for what it really is and give it up. If that is still too difficult, try harder with:

6. Right Effort (sammā-vāyāma).

2. Vyāpāda: Ill-will

This covers all kinds of thoughts based on the desire to reject. They are accompanied by feelings of hostility, resentment and bitterness. These range from the merest irritation to full-blown hatred resulting in physical violence, wars and genocides.

It forms a pair with Sensory Desire.

On the surface, this seems to make it the opposite of the first hindrance, which is based on energy that manifests as desire.

But, if that were the case, the opposite would be the absence of energy manifesting as anything at all. Just as turning off the hot tap doesn't mean cold water coming out, it means no water comes out at all, whether hot or cold.

Our spaceman doesn't just say, "No thank you!" and wind up the window when a native vendor offers to sell him a local souvenir. He leans out through the open window grabs him, and swears at him.

As a hindrance, Ill-will can be "external," towards others. "They shouldn't be allowed to sell such rubbish!"

Or "internal," Ill-will towards ourselves, "I hate myself for behaving like that towards someone trying to make a living!"

Sense-desire (kāma-chanda), the first mental hindrance, collects and holds on to what we consider pleasurable and right.

Ill-will (vyāpāda) does the opposite. It collects and holds on to those things we consider unpleasurable and wrong.

Kāma-chanda induces us to seek pleasure and truth outside of ourselves.

Vyāpāda deludes us into believing that the truth is in us and that we are right. So, we are unable to rise above ourselves even to the degree of respecting others. Anger is an intensification of ill-will.

Vyāpāda is always present, at least in latent form, when kāma-chanda is present.

Vyāpāda enshrouds us with a thick cloud of denial. We live in a private and limited mental world of our own creating and surround ourselves with an external world which mirrors it. We deny everything and anything we perceive that threatens our views and what we like.

Vyāpāda prevents or retards spiritual growth in a powerful way. Spiritual growth depends on the impartial and honest pursuit of Truth.

The Ego doesn't look in order to see what is actually there. It looks in order to see if what the Ego actually wants or doesn't want is there; and reacts accordingly.

3. Thīna-Middha: Sloth and Torpor

Thīna is a lack of motivating power in the mind.

Middha is a corresponding lack of motivating energy in the body.

The two go together. With Sloth, a deliberate attempt is being made to shut out the world by dimming the senses; eyes half-closed, mental earplugs in the ears. With Torpor, sedatives, inadequate exercise and excessive food provide the physical breeding ground to encourage Sloth.

Dullness in the mind means the physical senses are diminished. This leads to inadequate attention to the body's needs. This means increasing Slothfulness.

Together, heaviness of body and dullness of mind drag one down into a disabling inertia and thick depression.

At its extreme, one is totally at effect and unable to motivate oneself in any way. Health deteriorates. The next stage is diminishing consciousness. This is a state closer to death than sleep. The senses are gradually switched off, often with the drugs or alcohol which can accompany/cause sloth and torpor.

4. Uddhacca-Kukkucca: Restlessness and Regret

Uddhacca: excitement, restlessness. It is like water whipped up by the wind. It causes the mind to fly from one thought to another, often rushing around in circles.

Kukkucca (lit.) 'wrongly-performed-ness' (ku + krta + ya). Regret, remorse, uneasiness of conscience or worry. This results from having done something wrong; or even just regret at something that went wrong from our point of view.

It is a state of mind which is agitated and scattered. The image often given is of a layer of dust which has been stirred up or a bowl of still water into which more water is poured so that ripples go out in all directions.

Whenever the mind is working, it is moving. This in itself is not a problem.

What creates the Hindrance is when it is moving out of control. This one discovers when one tries to stop it. Since "mind comes first" and everything which is to be done starts with mind, one cannot overestimate the seriousness of the consequences of mind being out of control.

When one says mind is "out of control", one usually means it is out of one's own control. But the dust doesn't stir itself up. Nor does the water agitate itself. So, what is controlling the mind?

Associative thinking (one thought leading to another), feelings, memories, desires, sense objects appearing at the sense doors (one hears something or sees something or smells something or one's body itches or hurts). The list is endless. Many things can (and do) take control of what one thinks of as one's own mind.

With Kukkucca, Regret, uneasy conscience, the mind compulsively dwells on (grasps after) the past. It endlessly replays events and experiences whose roots lie in dissatisfaction.

But the past cannot be changed. Actions are only possible in present time. In the present, one can deal with the karmic consequences of those past events and/or learn from one's mistakes or those of others, and thereby create a different future.

But just dwelling on the past creates restless and morbid mental states which take control of the mind.

Together, Restlessness and Regret create a state of continual and uncontrollable unease which promotes action, not because actions are required, but because one cannot remain inactive in mind and body.

Anything that is done in this state is liable to have results which are unsatisfactory for oneself and others.

At its most extreme, one can become totally at effect and unable to restrain oneself in any way. It leads to hyper-consciousness. One cannot sleep. The senses cannot be switched off. Sometimes, a fuse is blown somewhere and one lapses into unconsciousness.

This is why one so rarely moves smoothly towards an intended goal. It is as though one sets off to drive somewhere but a host of other people keep trying to grab the steering wheel and steer off in different directions.

Restlessness and Regret, Uddhacca and Kukkucca, are also a hindrance to meditation. One can't make progress in meditation if one can't stop the mind drifting off the meditation object.

Even if one is not a meditator, the pressure that builds up under the momentum of constant restlessness and changes of direction results in stress. This stress makes one's life and relationships dysfunctional.

So, whether one is a meditator or just someone who wants to bring his mind under control in ordinary everyday life, it is essential to deal with this Hindrance.

There are two ways of doing this, both requiring perseverance.

The first is Concentration. One focuses the mind on a single, chosen object. The image given is of tying an animal to a post until it stops trying to run away. It then lies down peacefully.

The second is Investigation. One patiently undertakes

the task of observing the mind and its workings from moment to moment, in order to thoroughly understand how it operates. One's growing understanding is then used to gradually bring it under control.

It is essential to make certain that one's Ethics are firmly in place. This ensures that one no longer does, in the present, those things which are likely to become causes of Restlessness and Regret in the future.

Both methods require patience and perseverance. But the rewards of success are enormous. Even for everyday life.

Some people find it easier than others. This is because the more one has neglected one's mind, the harder it is to put it to rights.

If a gardener goes off for a few years, what he finds when he comes back will appear daunting. "Nature" has taken over.

Neglect of one's mind may have lasted much longer than a few years! Karma is perfect.

Just as Sensory Desire and Ill-Will make a pair, so do Sloth & Torpor and Restlessness & Regret also make a pair.

What they have in common is shutting down your awareness of things you do not want and do not want to see. With Sloth and Torpor this is obvious.

But even hyper-excitability is an inability or unwillingness to see what is actually presenting itself to the five senses.

You are so busy excitedly abusing the unfortunate vendor that you just don't notice that he has been replaced by the local policeman.

Sloth & Torpor and Restlessness & Regret are also opposites from the point of view of outward moving energy.

Sloth & Torpor indicates a deficiency of energy reaching out.

The one in the spaceship is slumped in his seat, half asleep, with the windows closed and curtains drawn.

Restlessness & Regret indicate an excess of energy reaching out.

The spaceman can't sit still, jumps frantically up and down all the time until he collapses, exhausted, in his seat.

5. Vicikicchā: Doubt

Vicikicchā literally means "the urge to think about". The prefix *vi-* has a sense of duality or separation, and *cikicchā* comes from the verb form, *cikicchāti* "he thinks about, bends towards, intends". *Vicikicchati*, is often translated as "he doubts."

Vicikicchā, Doubt, also appears as the second of the Ten Fetters (Saŋyojana).

Buddhists usually translate it as a lack of confidence in the Dhamma and doubt about the Buddha's teaching. It certainly includes this doubt. But it actually refers to <u>any</u> doubts.

Therefore, it applies to all human beings, Buddhists or not, who manifest mental wavering and instability.

Until one has completely freed oneself from all attachment to existence, one will constantly have doubts about all kinds of things which are part and parcel of existence: livelihood, the ways of the world, relationships, the past and the future.

But all these are things that exist only in the Sangsāra, the endless wandering on from birth to death.

It is like living in a prison, with one's attention entirely involved in activities within the prison. Should one paint the walls, change the curtains, install carpets, rearrange the room, make improvements, complain to the management?

Once one is convinced that it is a prison, that it is not a place to linger in, and that one is holding the exit key in one's hand, all one's doubts disappear and one makes straight for the door to escape. Once and for all.

But, until one is convinced, doubt remains.

This state has the nature of wavering. It appears as indecision and a divided attitude towards many things. It is associated with the tendency of the Ego not to want to consider anything which might disturb the laziness of its comfort zone.

It is lack of the mental energy (desire) to think things through and come to a conclusion.

Often it is accompanied, alternately, by Nos. 3 (Sloth and Torpor) and 4 (Restlessness).

It prevents the mind from resting and becoming peaceful. It hinders both sleep at night and the ability to deal with the challenges of waking life by day. It is a major obstacle in meditation.

The remedy is:

1. Developing concentration so that the mind doesn't rush around like a butterfly.

2. Unprejudiced and continuous investigation into the nature and workings of all things including the mind.

3. Careful and continuous observation of basic Sila, Ethics. This normalises one's relationship with other beings and one's environment. One no longer thinks, says and does things which have undesirable and unsettling consequences.

CONCLUSION

The Digha and Majjhima Nikāyas contain the fullest exposition of what the early Buddhists considered the original teachings of the Buddha to have been. The importance of the Hindrances is put in their context here.

A typical and comprehensive example, in the Digha, is the Samañña-Phala Sutta, The Fruits of the Life of a Recluse. *(See Appendix)*

It tracks, in great detail, the progress of a disciple from his first "going forth" from the life of a householder. It lists the methodical stages of practice, realisations and attainments, catalogued by the Buddha. This culminates in his ultimate arrival at the state of being of the Arahant; the one who has achieved the final state of permanent release from continual rebirth in the Sangsāra.

The Sangsāra

The Sangsāra is the endless wandering on from birth to death; the state of suffering and unsatisfactoriness in which all beings are immersed until they escape. It stretches from the lowest hells to the highest heavens. The inhabitants of our world, humans, animals, right down to microscopic beings, are sandwiched somewhere in between.

Escape

The path begins when "a householder or a man of inferior birth" hears the truth about suffering: its universality; its cause; its end; and the path and practice that leads to that final end of all suffering.

This seeker after Truth realises, "Full of Hindrances is a household life, a path for the dust of passion."

He gives up his attachment to the possessions and concerns of this world.

He practises self-restraint with regard to Ethics (Sila). He adopts and trains himself in the basic precepts, beginning with "Putting an end to the killing of living beings."

Firmly established in this, his conscience is clear and he has no fear of any beings he may encounter. "He experiences, within himself, a sense of unalloyed ease."

He is guarded with regard to the senses and does not become "entranced" by sense objects. He does not allow his mind to grasp after sense objects in a way that might lead to attachment and disappointment.

He is mindful and self-possessed in thought, word and deed of everything, all the time, from moment to moment.

He is content with sufficient clothes to protect his body and sufficient food to keep his body going.

He is then free to concentrate on putting an end to hankering after the world and its contents, and on purifying his mind of the Hindrances.

He finds himself as freed from debt (ethics), rid of disease (unwholesome states of mind), out of prison (free from the shackles of cravings), a free man (liberated in mind), and secure (safe from future becoming).

"Gladness rises up within him when he realises this."

Having reached this state, he can attain the jhānas and he "fills his body with that ease which has no excitability in it."

Furthermore, based on these progressive states in meditation, he can develop the attainment of various kinds of Iddhis (supernormal powers). Each of which is "higher and sweeter than the last".

Finally, with the final and permanent extinction of the Hindrances, he achieves:

"This, O king, an immediate fruit of the life of a recluse, visible in this world, and higher and sweeter than the last. And there is no fruit of the life of a recluse, visible in this world, that is higher and sweeter than this."

In a word, Nibbāna.

APPENDIX

This discourse, The Fruits of the Life of a Recluse (Samañña-Phala Sutta), was delivered to King Ajātasattu, one full moon, at his first meeting with the Buddha.

Ajātasattu was the son of King Bimbisara. He had his father imprisoned and killed, in order to obtain his kingdom.

After hearing this discourse, he saw the error of his ways and became a strong devotee of the Buddha, the Dhamma and the Sangha.

He erected a large Stupa for the bones and ashes of the Buddha after his funeral. He was present at the first Buddhist council at the Sattapanni Rock Cave in Rajagaha.

Ajātasattu was murdered by his own son, who was greedy for his kingdom.

A classic, historical, example of Karma.

CPSIA information can be obtained
at www.ICGtesting.com
Printed in the USA
BVHW052148260822
645599BV00008B/1128